Tricia Jackson, (Personnel Management), MInstAM,
FCIPD is a freelance training and personnel consultant.
Tricia has many years' experience as a generalist practi-
tioner in both the public and private sectors. She is currently involved in identifying and providing training solutions, personnel consultancy, tutoring on open learning
and college-based CIPD programmes and competence
assessment. Tricia is the co-author of the CIPD's recommended textbook for the Certificate in Personnel Practice
(*Personnel Practice*, M. Martin and T. Jackson, 2nd edn, CIPD,
2000) and also writes training videos (*Grievance and Disciplinary*
Procedures, 1998, Gower; and *Managing Your Own*
Career Development (2000). Tricia lives in Weybridge, Surrey.

The Chartered Institute of Personnel and Development is the
leading publisher of books and reports for personnel and training
professionals, students, and all those concerned with the effective
management and development of people at work. For details of all
our titles, please contact the Publishing Department:

tel 020-8263 3387

fax 020-8263 3850

e-mail publish@cipd.co.uk

The catalogue of all CIPD titles can be viewed on the CIPD website:

www.cipd.co.uk/publications

HANDLING GRIEVANCES

TRICIA JACKSON

Chartered Institute of Personnel and Development

Design and typesetting by
Wyvern 21, Bristol

Printed in Great Britain by the Short Run Press, Exeter

British Library Cataloguing-in-Publication Data
A catalogue record for this book is available
from the British Library

ISBN 0-85292-885-8

The views expressed in this book are the author's own and
may not necessarily reflect those of the CIPD.

Chartered Institute of Personnel and Development, CIPD House,
Camp Road, London SW19 4UX
Tel: 020-8971 9000 Fax: 020-8263 3333
E-mail: cipd@cipd.co.uk
Website: www.cipd.co.uk
Incorporated by Royal Charter. Registered charity no. 1079797.

Contents

Acknowledgements

Forgive the long list of names below, but many people have helped me in my research for this book. Some have been extremely generous with their time in patiently answering my queries and providing insights into their organisational practices. They and others, including many personal contacts, have provided me with their pearls of wisdom and a wealth of case study materials. I am only sorry that I have not been able to use them all.

My grateful thanks to all of the following:

George Boyce, Bernard Style, Mike Walsh and Richard Wilsher of ACAS, Louise Hill and Gareth Parry of Remploy, Norma French of Barnet & Chase Farm NHS Hospitals Trust, Lloyd Bryson of NCH Action for Children, Linda Dickinson and Julie Price of Ipswich Borough Council, John Dodge of Orion Cleaning Co. Ltd, Lin Riddet of Mexborough Citizens Advice Bureau, Christine Tebbutt and Kay Dixon of Catalyst (HR) Ltd, Barry Warne of Irwin Mitchell, Andrea Armstrong, Ken Baylis, Graham Boston, George Dow, Richard Jacobi, Lisa Pacey Wonnacott, Sheila Seabourne and Peter Winfield, and numerous other personal contacts who, sometimes unknowingly, have provided me with useful anecdotes and ideas.

What constitutes a grievance?

- ☑ Introduction
- ☑ Who should read this book?
- ☑ What are grievances?
- ☑ Examples of grievances and related procedures
- ☑ Individual v collective matters

Introduction

It is an inevitable fact that, from time to time, employees will feel disgruntled about aspects of their working lives. This may be due to the behaviour of work colleagues, the attitude of managers, the operation of a company policy, thwarted ambitions and a whole host of other reasons. If the culture within the organisation is such that employees feel that there is no means of raising their concerns, then these issues are unlikely ever to be resolved. There are a variety of likely outcomes, one of which is that employees become more and more discontented and ultimately may decide to leave. Exit interviews may reveal the real reasons for their departure, though this is often not the case. Even where employees do 'tell all' at the exit interview, it is usually too late to do anything about their complaint and ask them to reverse their decision.

Employers therefore need to have well-written grievance procedures in place that encourage employees to raise their complaints without fear of reprisal. Further, they need to ensure that when grievances are raised, they are handled sensitively and effectively. A fact that managers often seem to forget is that it takes some courage to 'raise your head above the parapet' and make a complaint. The reception that employees receive when they have made a stand is crucial to the maintenance of a healthy employment relationship and employee relations in general. Thus managers should welcome and encourage grievances rather than viewing them as an interruption to the job.

In this chapter we will be examining what we mean by the term 'grievance', the types of issues that may result in the raising of formal grievances, the fact that these issues may affect individual employees or employees collectively and whether grievances on specific issues are appropriately dealt with under grievance or other related workplace procedures.

In Chapter 2 we consider why organisations need formal procedures to deal with grievances. This is linked to the legal obligations on employers, which is covered in Chapter 3. In later chapters we look at the design and implementation of grievance policies and procedures and highlight good practices in conducting grievance investigations and interviews.

We will be emphasising the need to ensure that grievances are handled effectively so that problems can be quickly 'nipped in the bud' rather than be allowed to deteriorate into more serious disputes. Real case studies will be used throughout the book to demonstrate the key learning points.

Who should read this book?

This book has been written from the viewpoint of the organisation, but recognises the importance of taking account of the individual perspective. This is especially important in grievance procedures as grievances are initiated by employees or workers and are often the result of an individual's interpretation of events.

The book is primarily aimed at those who are responsible for formulating and reviewing grievance procedures and those who handle complaints and grievances in the workplace. This is likely to include line managers, from team leaders and supervisors to the most senior posts of managing directors and chief executives, as well as personnel specialists, trade union/employee representatives and other third parties. The book should also prove useful to individuals who are seeking to raise a grievance in the workplace and who want to understand more about the procedure and their rights.

What are grievances?

Employees become concerned or worried about all sorts of issues, some are workplace-related and others are of a more personal nature but may impact on their work situation. When they voice these concerns to managers, in order to seek some sort of redress, we tend to classify them initially as complaints. Good day-to-day management should ensure that the majority of such matters are

3

resolved quickly and to the satisfaction of all concerned parties.

It is not, however, always possible to find quick and easy solutions to employees' complaints. Further, there are a number of reasons why employees may be dissatisfied with the treatment they receive and/or the outcome of their complaint. For instance, employees may feel that:

- the manager was unapproachable and unwilling to take the complaint seriously
- there was a failure to analyse the true cause of the problem
- the proposed solution was a 'short-term fix' only
- the treatment they received would make them wary of raising future grievances.

There are a number of possible results for employees, including the following:

- They accept this unsatisfactory outcome and try to forget about the matter.
- They brood on the outcome and become disenchanted and demotivated.
- They decide to 'fight' the decision and pursue the complaint as a grievance.

In this book, 'grievances' will usually mean complaints that have been formally registered in accordance with the grievance procedure. We would suggest that when managers know that individuals are not satisfied with the response given to their complaints they should actively encourage them to formalise their concerns by registering a grievance. Employers should not view a low incidence of formal grievances as a sign of a contented workforce. The statistics may well be masking serious employee relations problems where workers feel that raising grievances is not worth the effort. (Chapter 2 covers the wider employee relations implications of poorly handled complaints and grievances.)

Examples of grievances and related procedures

The following are examples of issues likely to be raised as grievances within most organisations, both large or small:

- working environment, eg light, heat, space
- use of equipment, eg tools that have not been properly maintained
- supervisory practices, eg workload allocation
- personality clashes and other inter-employee disputes (work-related or otherwise)
- behaviours exhibited by managers or other employees, eg the allocation of 'perks' such as Sunday overtime working, and harassment, victimisation and bullying incidents
- refused requests, eg annual leave, shift changes
- problems with pay, eg late bonus payments, adjustments to overtime pay
- perceived inequalities in treatment, eg claims for equal pay, appeals against performance-related pay awards
- organisational change, eg the implementation of revised company policies or new working practices.

The range of issues included within the scope of grievance procedures varies from one workplace to the next. Smaller establishments may have to deal with all of the above matters and those listed below under their grievance procedures. On the other hand, more sophisticated or larger organisations may have in place alternative consultation arrangements or appeals mechanisms to deal with complaints about:

- disciplinary action
- health and safety issues
- job evaluation appeals or regrading applications
- sickness absence dismissals
- selection for redundancy
- catering matters
- discrimination, harassment or bullying allegations (possibly including claims that are not currently covered by statute, eg sexual orientation)
- operation of workplace policies, such as smoking or drugs and alcohol policies
- negotiated pay deals
- terms and conditions.

What do we mean by alternative arrangements or mechanisms? With regard to disciplinary cases, it is generally considered to be good practice to separate grievance and disciplinary procedures, as their aims are very different (see Chapter 3 for further discussion of this important point).

Other related mechanisms include policies and procedures for dealing with job evaluation appeals and regrading applications, discrimination, bullying and harassment allegations (including codes of conduct regarding the use of e-mail and intranets) and other workplace rules. There may also be committees or bodies set up for the purposes of discussing issues such as health and safety, catering mat ters and sickness absence management.

Pay and terms and conditions are more complex matters, which may be subject to separate negotiating arrange- ments (involving trade unions, staff associations or in- dividuals). Thus complaints about the levels of pay would be pursued through these negotiating mechanisms but concerns about late payment or unfair treatment in remuneration would be raised via the grievance procedure (see below for further information on disputes procedures).

Further, organisations may have in place a separate procedure designed to encourage employees, who wish to disclose issues of public interest, to raise such matters internally before resorting to external bodies such as the media. (See Chapter 3 for more information on the Public Interest Disclosure Act 1998.)

Decisions on the scope of the grievance procedure need to be made at the design or revision stage and will depend on the size, nature and culture of the organisation as well as how sophisticated its existing procedures are. Managers and personnel specialists will need to be familiar with the range of related procedures and mechanisms in order to be able to advise employees on the most suitable route to use when they wish to raise a grievance.

Individual v collective matters

For the purposes of this book, we will mainly be con- centrating on grievances that affect individual workers, but employers may also need to deal with grievances that affect groups of workers, ie collective grievances. Collective grievances can occur when individual grievances have a collective implication or when a group of workers has a dispute relating to their employment. An example of the former would be the refusal of an employee to accept a planned change to his or her shift-working arrangements as the resultant decision would have implications for all the other employees whose working patterns were also being changed. An example of the latter would be a dispute by a team of workers over the operation of bonus arrangements.

We have seen above that the scope of grievance procedures will vary depending on the size (and sophistication) of organisations. It will also depend on whether the organisation recognises a trade union with negotiating power over issues such as pay and terms and conditions of employment. Unionised organisations are likely to have in place disputes procedures that provide a process for dealing with concerns shared by groups of employees. However, as noted above, an individual grievance, if badly handled or unresolved, may have implications for other workers. Feelings may run so high that industrial action is the result. Some organisations may choose to have joint grievance and disputes procedures (see Appendix 1 for an example) and others may decide on separate procedures for dealing with individual and collective matters. (See Chapter 4 for more information on the contents of grievance procedures.)

Why do we need a formal procedure?

- ✔ Benefits
- ✔ Aims and objectives
- ✔ Poor handling of grievances
- ✔ The message
- ✔ Reference

Benefits

It is obvious that fair and efficient handling of complaints and grievances in the workplace can significantly contribute to good employee relations. Admittedly this can be achieved by good management practices alone but it is generally preferable to adopt a formal written policy and procedure, to ensure consistency and a co-ordinated approach. Another benefit is that should things go wrong, and a poorly handled grievance leads to an employment tribunal claim of constructive dismissal, the employer will have a better defence if it can be shown that a comprehensive grievance procedure was in place and was correctly utilised. (The legal requirements are covered in Chapter 3.)

In addition, the existence of formal grievance procedures should:

- encourage employees to raise concerns without fear of reprisal
- provide a fair and speedy means of dealing with complaints
- prevent minor disagreements developing into more serious disputes
- save employers time and money as solutions are found for workplace problems
- help to build an organisational climate based on openness and trust.

Terry Deegan[1] says it is important that a grievance procedure should not be tokenist in intent:

> Clearly, how the grievance procedure is perceived and applied are crucial issues. It is vitally important for the procedure to have credibility. All parties need to be satisfied that it is both fair in conception and application. It certainly should not be seen as a device for simply going through the motions. Neither should managers fear that it provides a stick for a disgruntled employee to beat them with. If a grievance is raised then it is crucial that all parties have a desire to ensure that there is a fair hearing of the complaint and that, ultimately, justice is done.

Aims and objectives

The aim of a grievance procedure is to provide a framework for dealing promptly and fairly with employee complaints that have not been resolved satisfactorily in the course of day-to-day working relationships. Thus, in providing a formal grievance procedure, employers recognise the right of employees to seek redress for grievances relating to their employment. Further, there is a desire to give fair consideration to all grievances and, where possible, to resolve them quickly and locally and to the satisfaction of all concerned.

With regard to collective grievances, the aim is to resolve workplace problems and prevent them developing into disputes. Disputes procedures should not just be viewed as a means of deflecting or avoiding conflicts, but as a vehicle for reconciling any differences between the parties to the employment relationship.

The objectives of a grievance procedure are to:

- enable the employee to air his or her grievance
- clarify the nature of the grievance
- investigate the reasons for dissatisfaction
- obtain, where possible, a speedy resolution to the problem
- take appropriate actions and ensure that promises are kept
- inform, in the event of an unsuccessful resolution, the employee of his or her right to take the grievance to the next stage of the procedure.

Poor handling of grievances

What if employees feel that managers have failed to respond to their grievances or have handled them badly? There are a number of potential outcomes, including:

- discontent and demotivation
- poor performance
- reduced productivity
- disciplinary issues
- increased labour turnover
- withdrawal of goodwill
- industrial action
- employment tribunal applications
- damage to the organisation's reputation
- resistance to change.

The last four points are explained in detail below.

1   Industrial action – this generally applies only to unionised environments and industrial action, or the threat of industrial action, may be the ultimate outcome if managers misjudge the strength of feeling behind a grievance.
2   Employment tribunal applications – these will mainly concern alleged breaches of contract and/or constructive dismissal claims. (See Chapter 3 for more information.)
3   Damage to the company's reputation – a well-publicised employment tribunal case can have a detrimental impact on the reputation of an employing organisation, notwithstanding the merits of the case and its outcome. Further, nowadays employers should be even more concerned about the effect on their public image as technology, particularly the Internet, allows employees and ex-employees to disseminate information about organisations speedily and very publicly, regardless of its validity.

4 Resistance to change – if employees feel that they have been badly treated they are more likely to be resistant to proposed changes. Further, many collective grievance (or disputes) procedures contain 'status quo' clauses. This means that, until all the stages of the procedure have been exhausted, management are prohibited from introducing changes. (See Chapter 4 for more detail.)

The message

The message is clear. Employers have a duty to provide their employees with a means to raise workplace-related issues as grievances and, if employers wish to establish and maintain good employee relations, they should respond to those grievances swiftly and effectively. This does not mean that the aim of grievance procedures is always to provide the solution that the employee is seeking but, where this is not possible, managers should be trained to act appropriately. This may involve counselling employees, seeking compromises or simply persuading employees that a change is not possible and supporting them in coping with this news. (See Chapter 6 for more details of the skills and knowledge required by managers in handling grievances.)

We shall see in Chapter 3 that there have recently been changes to the legal requirements placed on employers in grievance handling and new guidance has been provided by the Advisory, Conciliation and Arbitration Service (ACAS) in a revised Code of Practice. Further, the working environment in the twenty-first century is a very complex one and employers have to deal with a wide range of issues, such as harassment, bullying, Internet usage and whistleblowing, which previously received less prominent coverage.

Organisations without formal written grievance procedures are strongly advised to introduce them and all others should revise their existing procedures in the light of the new legislation and ACAS Code of Practice. (In Chapters 4 and 5 we provide further guidance on the design and implementation stages.)

Reference

1 DEEGAN T. *Croner's Records and Procedures: Employment Digest Briefing.* Croner CCH Group Ltd, Issue No. 511, 8 June 2000. p4.

What rights and duties does the law provide?

- ✔ The legal position

    Employment Rights Act 1996

    Implied term of contract

    Employment Relations Act 1999

    ACAS Code of Practice

    Natural justice

    Contractually binding procedures
- ✔ Employment rights
- ✔ Overlap with disciplinary procedures
- ✔ Associated legislation

    Employment Rights (Dispute Resolution) Act 1998

    Public Interest Disclosure Act 1998

    Data Protection Act 1998
- ✔ References

The legal position

Employers are not specifically required by law to have grievance procedures. Nevertheless, there are a number of strong legal arguments to support the case for formal grievance procedures within all employing organisations. The

15

following is an examination of the provisions of relevant statutes, codes and implied contract terms.

Employment Rights Act 1996

The Employment Rights Act 1996 requires employers to provide employees with a written statement specifying the main terms and conditions of their employment. These particulars must include reference to the person to whom the employee can apply to seek redress for any grievance relating to his or her employment and the manner in which the application should be made. The grievance procedure itself does not have to be provided as part of the statement but the document should be reasonably accessible to the employee.

Implied term of contract

Even where an employer fails to issue written particulars or does not include reference to the grievance procedure, an employee is still covered by an implied term in the contract of employment that the employer will provide a means of seeking redress for grievances. Failure to do so will amount to a breach of this implied term, entitling the employee to resign.

This right was established by the Employment Appeal Tribunal (EAT) in the case of *W A Goold (Pearmak) Ltd* v *McConnell* 1995 IRLR 516. Mr McConnell and a colleague were jewellery salesmen who were paid a basic salary plus commission. In 1992 the sales methods changed and their commission dropped considerably. Mr McConnell and his colleague tried, in the absence of a grievance procedure, to resolve the matter first by approaching their manager and then the new managing director. They were told that nothing could be done immediately. They then, having tried but failed to see the company chairman, resigned and claimed constructive dismissal.

The EAT supported the tribunal's finding of unfair dismissal and said:

> It is an implied term of the contract of employment that the employer will reasonably and promptly afford a reasonable opportunity to their employees to obtain redress of any grievances they may have.

Employment Relations Act 1999

The Employment Relations Act 1999 requires employers to permit workers to be accompanied at specified disciplinary and grievance meetings. This clause came into effect on 4 September 2000.

In summary, the main provisions in relation to grievances are as follows:

- The right extends to workers and not just employees working under a contract of employment. Thus self-employed people who do not run their own business, homeworkers and agency workers will also be included.
- The right applies to a grievance hearing 'which concerns the performance of a duty by an employer in relation to a worker'. The section on the ACAS Code below provides some clarification of what this means in practice but, at the time of writing, this area is the subject of much speculation.
- Workers will be protected against being victimised or dismissed in connection with this right, ie they

will be able to complain to employment tribunals of both unfair dismissal and detrimental treatment.

- The accompanying person may be a fellow worker, a full-time or lay trade union official. This right applies equally to workers in unionised and non-unionised environments.
- The employer may need to postpone the hearing if the chosen companion is not available.
- Fellow workers and lay trade union officials should be allowed a reasonable amount of paid time off to fulfil their duties.
- The chosen companion may address the hearing, ask questions and confer privately with the worker but has no legal right to answer questions on behalf of the worker.
- Failure to allow a worker to be accompanied or to rearrange a hearing to accommodate the worker's companion may result in a complaint to an employment tribunal and a compensation award of up to two weeks' pay. (See Chapter 4 for advice on how to incorporate this right into grievance procedures.)

Please note that in this book we will be using the terms employee and worker interchangeably, although they do have separate and specific meanings under employment law.

ACAS Code of Practice

The ACAS *Code of Practice on Disciplinary and Grievance Procedures* (2000) contains guidance on the statutory provisions above. Although a failure to follow the Code will not render an employer liable to any proceedings, the Code will be admissible in evidence and can be taken into account by employment tribunals.

This Code replaces the previous *Code of Practice on Disciplinary Practices and Procedures in Employment*. It retains many of the essential features listed as characterising a good disciplinary procedure but, as its name suggests, also provides detailed guidance on the operation of grievance procedures.

In particular, the Code provides assistance in deciding on the likely subject matter of grievance hearings to which the new right of accompaniment is applicable. ACAS interprets this as meaning those grievance hearings that concern the employer's contractual and statutory duties. In other words, the grievance can concern existing terms of contracts or legal duties but not the pursuit of improvements.

Thus on the balance of probabilities, the following examples would or would not attract the right to be accompanied:

Not applicable	Applicable
A complaint about the appearance of safety shoes	A complaint about the design of safety shoes not offering adequate protection (statutory provision and duty of care)
A request for a pay rise (in the absence of a contractual provision)	An equal pay claim (statutory provision)
A request for subsidised health care or a travel loan, where not previously provided	A complaint about the application of a grading or promotion exercise (contractual issues)
A request for car parking facilities, where not previously provided	A request for car parking facilities from a disabled worker (duty of care)
Minor disputes between fellow workers, eg personality clashes, day-to-day frictions	Complaints about bullying or harassment (duty of care)

A strict enforcement of such distinctions could easily become problematic (and a distraction from the process). This is especially the case where the real cause of a grievance is not immediately apparent and only comes to light during the investigations and/or grievance hearing(s). Case law will throw more light on this subject, but informed opinion suggests that employers should adopt a more flexible approach where accompaniment is allowed for all formal grievances. (This course of action is recommended in Chapter 4.)

The ACAS Code also provides guidance on the suitability of companions and reasonableness of requests by workers to be accompanied. Again, case law will have a final say in determining these issues, but essentially the following advice is given:

- Workers are free to choose any one fellow worker or trade union official, but workers 'should bear in mind that it would not be appropriate to insist on being accompanied by a colleague whose presence would prejudice the hearing or who might have a conflict of interest. Nor would it be sensible for a worker to request accompaniment by a colleague from a geographically remote location when someone qualified was available on site. The request to be accompanied need not be in writing.'[1]
- 'Workers are free to choose an official from any trade union to accompany them at a disciplinary or grievance hearing regardless of whether the union is recognised or not. However where a trade union is recognised in a workplace it is good practice for an official from that union to accompany the worker at a hearing.'[2]

Natural justice

In common with disciplinary procedures, grievance procedures need to adhere to the rules of natural justice. The basic tenets of natural justice are that:

- grievance procedures should be fair and should be seen to be fair
- there should be a full investigation by an unbiased individual to establish the facts of the case
- employees have a right to a fair and unbiased hearing
- employees who have raised a grievance should not subsequently be disadvantaged in any way.

The remaining chapters provide guidance on how to ensure that these points are covered, both in grievance procedures and management practices.

Contractually binding procedures

It should be noted that it is preferable for employers *not* to have contractually binding procedures. If the grievance procedure is incorporated in the contract of employment then all employees, regardless of length or continuity of employment, will be able to bring a breach of contract claim if the procedure has not been followed 'to the letter'. Thus employees with less than 12 months' service would not be able to claim constructive dismissal but would be entitled to put in a claim for damages for breach of contract to an employment tribunal. Further, once incorporated, the procedure would be difficult to change.

To avoid this, procedures should contain wording to this effect:

> This procedure is for guidance only and does not form part of the employee's contractual rights. Further, its contents may be revised from time to time.

Employment rights

There are a number of employment rights associated with the operation of grievance procedures. These are summarised below:

- Employees are entitled to a written statement of their main terms and conditions of employment, which should include a reference to the procedure for making a complaint.
- There is no statutory obligation for employers to provide a grievance procedure, but there is a clearly established implied term in the contract of employment.
- Failure by employers to provide a suitable mechanism for dealing with employees' complaints or to respond appropriately will result in breaches of contract (employees may therefore be entitled to resign and claim constructive dismissal).
- Workers have a statutory right to be accompanied to certain grievance hearings and companions have a right to a reasonable amount of paid time off for this purpose.
- Workers are protected against victimisation or dismissal in connection with the right of accompaniment.
- Other claims for breach of contract could arise when an employer fails to follow precisely a grievance procedure that has been incorporated into the contract of employment or fails to rearrange a grievance hearing when it becomes apparent that a suitable companion is not available.

Overlap with disciplinary procedures

What happens when grievances are raised at the same time as disciplinary issues?

In answering this question, we will first assume that, in line with good practice, employers have separate procedures for dealing with grievances and disciplinaries. Thus appeals against disciplinary decisions should be channelled through the disciplinary appeals procedure, not the grievance procedure.

However, an employee may wish to raise a grievance about the way in which a manager handled a disciplinary or conducted the investigation. An employee in this position has a right to seek redress even when facing disciplinary charges. Employers must therefore observe both sets of procedural rules. The ACAS Code provides the following advice:

> Where this happens and depending on the circumstances, it may be appropriate to suspend the disciplinary procedure for a short period until the grievance can be considered. Consideration might also be given to bringing in another manager to deal with the disciplinary case.[3]

Case study 1 provides a demonstration of these points.

Case study 1 – don't confuse disciplinary and grievance procedures

In a medium-sized enterprise the performance of a long-serving manager was starting to cause concern. The personnel manager decided to raise this matter in an informal discussion and discovered that the male manager was being harassed by one of his staff, a female clerk. He admitted that he had had an affair with the clerk but that it was now over. The harassment appeared to be of a serious nature and had, in the main, involved her telephoning him at home and threatening to tell his wife, as well as physically stalking him.

A decision was made to discipline the clerk and she was suspended on full pay, pending further investigations. She raised a formal grievance, complaining that she should not be disciplined over what was essentially a private matter.

The personnel manager considered that, though the majority of incidents had taken place outside of the work environment, others had occurred on company premises. She was also aware of the employer's duty of care to the manager, who appeared to be close to a nervous breakdown at this point. She decided to put the disciplinary procedure on hold and to arrange for the grievance to be heard by an independent party. It was not upheld and the clerk chose not to pursue it to the next stage. After the resumption of the disciplinary proceedings, the clerk was dismissed.

Associated legislation

Finally in this chapter, we consider three further pieces of legislation that have an impact on the design and operation of grievance procedures.

Employment Rights (Dispute Resolution) Act 1998

The Employment Rights (Dispute Resolution) Act 1998 covers the provision by ACAS of a voluntary arbitration scheme as an alternative mode of dispute resolution to employment tribunals, applicable initially to unfair dismissal claims only. In theory, constructive dismissal claims relating to workplace grievances may, subject to the agreement of both parties, be resolved by a process of voluntary arbitration.

At the time of writing, this scheme is in the early stages of development. (See Chapter 4 for further details of the various roles played by ACAS officers in dispute resolution and the potential for using external facilitators as part of the internal procedure, ie prior to employment tribunal claims.)

Public Interest Disclosure Act 1998

The Public Interest Disclosure Act 1998 provides further protection from dismissal or detriment for workers who legitimately raise concerns about certain workplace practices. Commonly known as the Whistleblowers Act, the term 'whistleblowing' is used to describe a situation where a worker perceives a wrongdoing at work and reports it to an outsider. The types of disclosure covered are:

- failure to comply with legal obligations
- miscarriages of justice

- health and safety risks
- environmental damage.

With regard to grievance procedures, the Act encourages workers to make the disclosure to the employer in the first instance. There are, therefore, two major options for employers:

1. Take account of these provisions in drafting a new grievance procedure by, for example, allowing individuals to raise their concerns at a higher stage in the procedure.
2. Draw up a separate 'whistleblowers' procedure to reflect the greater sensitivity and seriousness attached to such matters.

(See Chapter 7 for the contact details for Public Concern at Work, an independent charity working in this area.)

Data Protection Act 1998

The Data Protection Act 1998 has implications for grievance procedures in respect of record keeping. The ACAS Code states that:

> Records should be kept detailing the nature of the grievances raised, the employers response, any action taken and the reasons for it. These records should be kept confidential and retained in accordance with the Data Protection Act 1998 which requires the release of certain data to individuals on their request. Copies of any meeting records should be given to the individual concerned although in certain circumstances some information may be withheld, for example to protect a witness.[4]

References

1 ACAS. *Code of Practice on Disciplinary and Grievance Procedures.* S.56, p21. London, ACAS, 2000.
2 *Ibid.*, S.58, p22.
3 *Ibid.*, S.48, p18.
4 *Ibid.*, S.49, p18.

What should a grievance procedure contain?

- ✔ Main principles
- ✔ Policy statement
- ✔ Essential features
- ✔ Contents
- ✔ Notes
  - Note 1 – deadlines for action
  - Note 2 – individual v collective issues
  - Note 3 – disputes procedures/status quo clause
  - Note 4 – right of accompaniment
  - Note 5 – external facilitators
  - Note 6 – special allowances
  - Note 7 – small firms
- ✔ Example clauses
  - Recommended clauses
  - Optional clauses
  - Suggested appendices
- ✔ Presentation
- ✔ Roles played by ACAS officials and other third parties
- ✔ References

Main principles

There are no set rules regarding the contents of grievance procedures, but good practice dictates that procedures should be:

- set down in writing
- aimed at settling matters as closely as possible to the point of origin
- equitable in the way in which all workers are treated
- simple to understand
- rapid in their operation to ensure that grievances are processed in a timely manner.

Further, they should ensure that, if a grievance is not settled at the informal or first formal stage, workers have the right to have their grievances heard at further levels, ie the right of appeal should be built into each stage.

The number of stages contained in the procedure will vary depending on the size and nature of the organisation, the management structure and the availability of resources. ACAS[1] advises that grievance procedures should outline:

- how and with whom to raise the issue
- whom next to apply to if not satisfied
- time limits to each stage
- the right to be represented.

Policy statement

Organisations often introduce their grievance procedure with a statement of policy. This can be very useful in emphasising to employees the purpose of the grievance procedure and, perhaps more importantly, reminding managers of their role in dealing with grievances. A typical policy statement would refer to:

- the aim of the grievance procedure, ie to resolve grievances as quickly and as fairly as possible
- the scope of the grievance procedure, eg the types of issues that are dealt with under separate procedures and/or the fact that the grievance procedure does not cover appeals against disciplinary decisions. Further, it should be made clear which groups of workers are covered by the procedure, if there is more than one procedure in operation in your organisation.

See Section 1 of Appendix 1 for a useful example of a policy statement.

Essential features

Grievance procedures should:

- provide for proceedings and records to be kept confidential, in accordance with the Data Protection Act 1998. Employers must keep accurate records detailing the nature of the grievance, the management response and the reasons behind it, as well as any actions taken. (See *Case study 2* below regarding the need to provide full reasons for management decisions.)
- allow for the investigation and hearing of grievances to be dealt with by unbiased managers.

As is the case in disciplinary investigations and hearings, managers handling grievances need to be open-minded and impartial in their thoughts and actions.

- allow for individuals to be represented or accompanied at grievance hearings. (Similarly it is good practice to ensure that managers are accompanied by another management representative who can act as a witness and/or a note-taker.)
- be made known to all workers either by providing individual copies during induction or by providing access via, say, the organisation's intranet site. (Special allowances should be made for individuals with disabilities or whose first language is not English.) Further, training should be provided to managers and worker representatives to ensure that the system operates as smoothly as possible. (See Chapter 5 for more information on this aspect.)
- allow individuals the right to 'go to the top', ie provide the means for serious grievances to be heard, if not by the managing director or chief executive, by senior executives who have been authorised to act on behalf of the managing director or chief executive.
- in certain cases, encourage the use of external facilitators acting as conciliators, mediators or arbitrators. (See the section below on the potential role for third parties.)
- have built-in flexibility such that, though there is an obligation to deal with grievance issues

promptly, there is some leeway for agreeing extended deadlines. (See *Note 1* below.)

Case study 2 – explain your reasoning

In one small company, which was struggling to remain viable, a decision was made by the company chair to demote the managing director to general manager and take on more of the operational responsibilities herself. The managing director naturally reacted with some anger to this proposal. He stated that he wished to raise a formal grievance but felt that it would be fruitless because it would be heard by the company chair who could not be impartial.

The company chair tried to erase these fears and arranged the first of three formal meetings. The subsequent discussions did not always go smoothly but the company chair was able to convey her concerns about the company and the reasons behind this difficult decision, which was intended to help to preserve other jobs.

The managing director eventually accepted that this drastic step was necessary and volunteered to personally communicate the change to the rest of the staff, in an attempt to generate their commitment to turning the company's performance around.

Contents

Grievance procedures should conform to an upward hierarchical structure and allow for an informal stage as well as a number of formal stages. It is difficult to recommend one model procedure, so two template policies and procedures are provided to cover differing organisational circumstances. The two templates are designed to accommodate individual grievances and they highlight the differences between the arrangements in unionised and non-unionised environments. (For help in designing a collective procedure, see *Note 2* and *Note 3* below.)

Template 1 – A template grievance procedure for a non-unionised organisation

Introduction

It is the Company's policy to encourage workers with grievances relating to their employment to use the procedure below to seek satisfactory solutions. The Company will endeavour to resolve grievances as quickly as possible to the satisfaction of the individuals concerned. Where this is not possible, every effort will be made to explain the reasons for the decision and, where workers are not satisfied with the outcome, they have the right to pursue their grievance to the next stage. It is hoped that most grievances will be resolved during the informal discussions. Workers who have raised grievances will be treated fairly at all times before, during and after the conclusion of the grievance hearing(s).

Informal stage

If you have a grievance about your employment you should discuss it informally with your immediate manager.

Stage 1

If you feel that the matter has not been resolved satisfactorily through informal discussions, you should put your grievance in writing to your immediate manager. A meeting will be arranged and will be attended by yourself, any relevant witnesses and the manager. You may choose to be accompanied by a fellow worker, lay or trade union

---

official. The manager will give a response within five working days of the meeting.

Stage 2

If you are not satisfied with the manager's response, you may raise the matter, in writing, with the relevant senior manager. A meeting will be arranged, constituted as in Stage 1, except that the manager will be replaced by the senior manager. The senior manager will give a response within five working days of the meeting.

Stage 3

If the matter is not resolved to your satisfaction, you should put your grievance in writing to the managing director in order for a meeting to be arranged to discuss the matter. The constitution of the meeting will be as in Stage 2 except that the senior manager will be replaced by the managing director or his or her authorised deputy. The managing director or deputy will give his or her decision within seven working days of the meeting. This decision will be final.

Template 2 – A template grievance procedure for a unionised organisation

Introduction

It is the organisation's policy to ensure that everything possible is done by managers and workers to encourage and maintain good employee relations in order to ensure a motivated workforce and an efficient service. Thus where grievances arise, they will be dealt with fairly, speedily and as closely as possible to the point of origin. The organisation and trade union(s) have agreed the following grievance procedure to facilitate this process. Every effort will be made to ensure that all workers are aware of the procedure and that managers are trained to handle grievances efficiently and effectively.

Informal stage

If you have a grievance about your employment you should discuss it informally with your immediate manager.

Stage 1

If you feel that the matter has not been resolved satisfactorily through informal discussions, you may raise the matter formally, via a representative if you wish. You should put your grievance in writing to your immediate manager. A meeting will be arranged and will be attended by yourself, your representative, any relevant witnesses and the manager. The manager will give a response within five working days of the meeting.

Stage 2

If you are not satisfied with the manager's response, you or your representative may raise the matter, in writing, with the relevant senior manager. A meeting will be arranged, constituted as in Stage 1, except that the manager will be replaced by the senior manager. The senior manager will give a response within five working days of the meeting.

Stage 3

If the matter is not resolved to your satisfaction, you or your representative should put your grievance in writing to the chief executive in order for a meeting to be arranged to discuss the matter. The meeting will be attended by yourself, your representative or a local full-time union official (if applicable), any relevant witnesses and the chief executive or his or her authorised deputy. The chief executive or deputy will give his or her decision within seven working days of the meeting.

Stage 4

If the matter is not resolved to your satisfaction, ie there is a failure to agree, you have the right to refer the matter in writing to a Grievance Committee. A Committee will be convened, to include an independent chair nominated by ACAS, a non-executive director and a regional full-time union official. None of the Committee members will have had any previous involvement in the case. The matter will be considered through a formal hearing, which will be arranged within one calendar month of the receipt of the failure to agree. The decision of the Committee will be final.

Notes

The following notes provide additional information on the templates above and are relevant to the formulation of grievance procedures in general.

Note 1 – deadlines for action

Each stage should be timebound in order that a speedy resolution can be sought. Three to five working days' duration is the norm for the early stages, but more serious disputes, ie those that are pursued to the later stages of the procedure, may require considerably longer.

In any event, it is wise to build some flexibility into the process. This may be necessary where a case is particularly complex and requires further thought or investigation or where key witnesses are not available. A rider allowing both parties to agree to extensions to deadlines would help to ensure that decisions are not unduly hurried and regretted later.

Organisations may wish to put detailed time limits on the following events:

- receipt of the written grievance by the manager to convening the grievance interview
- the conclusion of the grievance interview to the manager's notification of the decision in writing to the worker
- the receipt of the notification by the worker to the deadline for referral to the next stage.

Note 2 – individual v collective issues

Employers may decide to distinguish between individual and collective grievances by providing two separate procedures or a joint procedure. In the former case, the collective grievance (or disputes) procedure is likely to contain fewer stages than the individual grievance procedure. In the latter case, there may be an allowance for matters affecting a group of workers to be raised with a higher level of management than is represented at Stage 1, ie to leapfrog the early stages of the procedure.

Note 3 – disputes procedures/status quo clause

Stage 4 of Template 2 refers to a situation where a final decision is taken by an independent committee. Many unionised organisations, however, will have in place arrangements such that the grievance procedure and the disputes procedure dovetail at this final stage. Thus one possible outcome of an individual or collective grievance is industrial action. However, no form of industrial action can be taken until all the stages have been completed and a failure to agree recorded, ie the disputes procedure has been exhausted.

Further, existing disputes procedures may include a 'status quo' clause. This is in recognition of the fact that grievances and disputes may arise from a management decision or action. As its name suggests, this is a provision whereby management is precluded from making any changes until agreement has been reached or a failure to agree has been processed to the final stage of the disputes procedure.

See Appendix 1 for an example of a joint grievance and disputes procedure.

Note 4 – right of accompaniment

Chapter 3 summarised the worker's right to be accompanied at certain grievance hearings. However, until case law provides clearer guidance on the extent of this right, a cautious approach is recommended. Thus, bearing in mind the provisions of the Employment Relations Act 1999 and the ACAS *Code of Practice on Disciplinary and Grievance Procedures* (2000), it would be sensible to:

- notify all workers of their right to be accompanied at *all* formal grievance hearings by suitable persons
- consider requests for accompaniment in the light of the suitability of the chosen companion and the reasonableness of the request, eg a trained lay official from the trade union recognised by the organisation
- allow companions to participate as fully as

possible in the hearing, ie not restrict their role unduly, and allow time for the companion to confer privately with the worker.

For further details on this right, refer directly to the ACAS Code.

Note 5 – external facilitators

In some circumstances it might be helpful to seek assistance from an external facilitator. This would be especially relevant where, say, the complaint is against the managing director or chief executive or where relationships have broken down. Experience has shown that differing forms of alternative dispute resolution often prove to be very powerful tools. (See *Case study 3* for an example of this and the section below on the role of ACAS and other third parties for more information.)

Case study 3 – make use of external facilitators

In one organisation a restructuring programme led to a number of employees being classified as 'displaced'. The personnel officer offered one manager a choice of two possible positions, without first consulting the appropriate department heads. Unfortunately, the manager favoured one position much more than the other and was very annoyed to be told subsequently that the department head wanted to openly advertise the vacancy. The manager failed to secure this position and reluctantly accepted his second choice. He pursued a grievance about the treatment he had received but was dissatisfied with the response he received at each stage. At the final stage, in view of the deteriorating

---

employment relationship, a process of independent mediation was agreed.

The result was that the manager remained in the new job, having been convinced that the organisation valued his skills and expertise and that there was potential for further progression. He also received a small pay rise and a written apology.

Note 6 – special allowances

Special allowances should be made for individuals whose first language is not English or who have a disability such as visual impairment. It would be advisable to discuss what arrangements are needed with the individuals themselves (as this might have a bearing on the role played by the companion).

Note 7 – small firms

Small firms may only have the facilities to provide a one or two stage procedure. The ACAS Code[2] recommends that 'where there is only one stage, for instance in very small firms where there is a single owner/manager, it is especially important that the person dealing with the grievance acts impartially'. This is actually very difficult and small firms would be advised to consider using third parties to hear appeals against grievance (and disciplinary) decisions. Chapter 7 refers to an ACAS guide that has been specially written for small firms.

Example clauses

The following clauses can be adapted and included in your grievance procedure, depending on their suitability.

Recommended clauses

- This procedure is for guidance only and does not form part of employees' contractual rights. The contents may be subject to revision from time to time.
- A second management representative from the personnel department or another function will be invited to attend formal grievance interviews. This person will act as a witness and note-taker.
- Should your grievance be of a personal nature or directly concern your immediate manager, such that you are uncomfortable about raising it with your manager, you can initially raise the grievance with the personnel manager or a manager from another department.
- The timescales listed above will be adhered to wherever possible. However, where there are good reasons, eg the need for further investigation or the lack of availability of witnesses or companions, each party can request that the other agrees to an extension of the permitted timescale.

Optional clauses

- If the grievance remains unresolved at Stage 3 it may be referred to an external body for arbitration. The decision of the arbitrator will be final, though without prejudice to the parties' statutory rights and obligations.

● The scope of this grievance procedure is restricted to issues that are not covered by other company procedures such as the disciplinary procedure, job evaluation appeals procedure, the 'harassment at work' procedure and the 'dealing with public concerns (whistleblowing)' procedure. Please seek advice from the personnel department if you are unsure about which procedure to use.

● If the subject matter of your complaint is of a particularly sensitive nature, you may refer your grievance to a higher level of management, as depicted in the grievance procedure. Please seek advice from the personnel department if you are unsure about this.

Suggested appendices

You may also wish to consider providing further information as appendices to your procedure, eg a pro forma document for notification of a formal grievance, additional guidance on the procedure to be followed at the hearing (see Appendix 1 for examples of both) and guidance notes for managers, representatives/companions and workers (see Appendix 2 for an example employee checklist).

Presentation

By now you should be convinced of the need for a formal written grievance procedure and have some good ideas about the suitability of the contents. You have probably realised that the procedure, if it is to be comprehensive, will need to be reasonably lengthy. Thus, in terms of presentation, you might consider a flowchart format for the stages (see Appendix 3), as this provides a useful overview.

Roles played by ACAS officials and other third parties

The mission of ACAS is 'to improve the performance and effectiveness of organisations by providing an independent and impartial service to prevent and resolve disputes and to build harmonious relationships at work'.

ACAS has four main roles. It seeks to:

- prevent and resolve employment disputes
- conciliate in actual and potential complaints to employment tribunals
- provide information and advice
- promote good practice.

All of these roles are relevant to the handling of workplace grievances, so potentially ACAS has a substantial contribution to make in helping to resolve individual and collective grievances.

But what involvement does ACAS have in internal grievance procedures? In practice, the emphasis, in terms of resource allocation, is very much centred on collective issues. ACAS activities include giving advice, voluntary conciliation, mediation and arbitration. The main differences between these activities are that:

- in *conciliation*, the conciliator (an ACAS official)

attempts, through informal discussion, to help the parties to reach their own agreement

- in *mediation*, non-binding proposals are put forward by the mediator (ACAS-appointed or an independent third party) for consideration by the parties
- in *arbitration*, the parties will have reached a prior agreement to be bound by the arbitrator's decision (here ACAS will appoint an independent arbitrator or a board of arbitration).

In practice, conciliation is often used as a first step before resorting to mediation or arbitration. It should be noted that, before considering requests for conciliation, mediation and arbitration, ACAS takes account of whether the internal disputes procedure has first been exhausted.

ACAS officers have a much more limited involvement in individual grievance cases, especially (and understandably) while internal procedures are still in operation. However, the network of public enquiry points will provide free advice to individuals and organisations involved in pursuing or responding to grievances. The picture changes when the employment relationship has come to an end and ACAS has a statutory duty to conciliate in actual and potential unfair dismissal claims to employment tribunals. The aim is to resolve the matter before it gets to a tribunal hearing via a settlement, withdrawal of the claim or an alternative solution, such as reinstatement.

What about other third parties? We mentioned above the option of providing a role for external facilitators in the later stages of the grievance (and/or disputes) procedure. This usually tends to be confined to collective issues, though could be equally valuable in dealing with individual matters. Third parties can include ACAS officials and ACAS-appointed or recommended independent mediators or arbitrators, plus other qualified mediators, lawyers, members of the council (for local authorities), advice centre workers, union officials and any other persons deemed by you to be suitably experienced and impartial. Such organisations as CEDR (Centre for Dispute Resolution) play a leading role here. (See Chapter 8 for the contact details.)

Finally, trade unions and Citizens Advice Bureaux (CABs) have extensive experience in advising individuals about their employment rights. CAB staff also provide advice to employers and, given adequate resources, may be willing to play a facilitating role in internal grievance procedures.

Further, if discrimination is involved, bodies such as the Commission for Racial Equality, Equal Opportunities Commission and the Disability Rights Commission may be called upon as another source of help and advice.

References

1 ACAS. *Self Help Guide on Producing Disciplinary and Grievance Procedures.* p11. London, ACAS, 1999.
2 ACAS. *Code of Practice on Disciplinary and Grievance Procedures.* S.44, p17. London, ACAS, 2000.

How do we make it work?

- ✔ Introduction
- ✔ Design and implementation
  - Audit existing arrangements
  - Consult the workforce
  - Pilot the procedure
  - Publicise the procedure
  - Provide training and guidance
  - Revise associated documentation
  - Integrate with other management activities
- ✔ Operating grievance procedures
- ✔ Monitoring and evaluation
- ✔ Reference

Introduction

This chapter will deal with the practicalities of operating a grievance procedure (the skills and knowledge aspects are covered in Chapter 6). We start with guidance on how to ensure the successful design and implementation of your new (or revised) grievance procedure. We then highlight good practice tips on operating a grievance procedure.

Finally, we stress the need to monitor and evaluate success. This is judged by assessing whether the procedure has achieved its aims. In general terms, this means looking at whether the new procedure enhances employee relations or whether it is seen as a management tool that merely pays lip service to employee involvement.

Design and implementation

Chapter 4 covered the possible contents of your new procedure and stated that this would depend on a number of factors. Thus it is important to ensure that the design:

- reflects the legislative requirements
- is suited to your organisational circumstances
- is workable.

Therefore, the following seven main stages of design and implementation are recommended:

1 Audit the existing arrangements.
2 Consult the workforce.
3 Pilot the new procedure.
4 Publicise the new procedure.
5 Provide training and guidance.
6 Revise associated documentation.
7 Integrate the procedure with other management activities.

Audit existing arrangements

As with most organisation-wide initiatives, the early establishment of a working party is a useful starting point. The working party should be drawn from all sectors and levels of the workforce and will be involved, to varying degrees, in all the stages below.

The first job is for the working party to audit the existing arrangements to answer such questions as:

- Does the existing procedure (written or unwritten) comply with current legislation?
- How accurate are existing records on grievances and grievance-related incidents?
- How easy is it to analyse this data?
- What are the views of managers and workers on the content and structure of the existing arrangements?
- Are these arrangements user-friendly?
- How many informal complaints have been received in the recent past?
- How many became formal grievances?
- How were these dealt with and by whom?
- At which stage of the existing procedure were they resolved?
- What are the most common causes of grievances?
- How quickly were grievances dealt with at each stage?
- What happened when there were 'failures to agree'?
- How many employment tribunal claims/industrial action incidents have emanated from grievances in the recent past?
- What other options, such as the use of external parties, could be considered for inclusion in the new procedure?

Consult the workforce

You may choose to use existing consultation mechanisms or set up alternatives in order to carry out consultation with the workforce. The main aim is to gauge views and generate suggestions from as broad a spectrum of your workers as possible. A number of the following methods or forums may be suitable:

- regular team/department meetings, including team briefings
- newsletters and the intranet
- questionnaires
- suggestion scheme
- discussions with trade union and other employee representatives
- working party discussions.

It is important to develop a procedure that is acceptable to those who are covered by its provisions and those who have to operate it. By ensuring a high profile for the consultation process you will be raising employee awareness of the need for a new grievance procedure and will be encouraging its future use.

Worker consultations should not be considered to have been completed at the end of this stage but should be viewed as a continuous process.

Pilot the procedure

Having taken account of a broad range of views, the final draft procedure should ideally be tested before it is formally adopted. You can pilot the new procedure either by working through a number of hypothetical situations or, ideally, by carrying out 'test runs' on actual cases. This process is necessary to ensure that the procedure is understandable, easy to use and that time limits are realistic.

The final procedure, amended as necessary, can then be agreed with the appropriate parties, before being publicised.

Publicise the procedure

Effective communication of the new or revised procedure is crucial. There are a number of options for you to choose from when publicising the new or revised procedure:

- Announce its introduction, aims and contents with a letter from the managing director or chief executive.
- Introduce the new procedure by carrying out a series of briefings for line managers, other key personnel and union/employee representatives.
- Display the new procedure on notice boards and/or the company intranet and issue copies to all workers.
- Reinforce the message via existing communication mechanisms, such as team briefings and internal newsletters.
- Change relevant procedures and the staff handbook to reflect the new procedure.
- Include discussion of the grievance procedure at induction.
- Continue the process by announcing 'successes', eg improved working methods that have resulted from grievances.

Provide training and guidance

The provision of training and guidance is an often-forgotten but extremely important stage. If line managers are not committed to making the new grievance procedure a success, or are unsure about their responsibilities, then good practices will not be consistently achieved. Training or coaching sessions should be arranged so that managers will be competent and confident in handling both individual and collective grievances.

Effective training and a supportive environment should encourage managers to 'own' the procedure but, as we will see in Chapter 6, handling grievances involves a large number of skills and knowledge requirements. You may decide to provide specific grievance training programmes, but existing training courses covering associated skills such as interviewing and counselling or general management should also be useful.

Ian Smith[1] provides a useful list of objectives for grievance training programmes. He says that, at the end of the training, managers should appreciate:

- how to listen to a complaint
- how to investigate a complaint
- how to properly document the investigation
- how to deal with sensitive issues, particularly those involving allegations of sexual or racial harassment, bullying or personal problems
- how to mediate
- how (and when) to resolve a matter informally and amicably where possible
- how to notify a complainant of the decision
- how to monitor compliance with any decision.

It should be noted that, as managers' involvement in griev-ance handling may be infrequent, refresher courses should be provided on a regular basis alongside employment law updates.

The provision of training may be extended to union and other employee representatives or companions (though trade unions often provide their own training). Workers too should not be forgotten and, though it may be unrealistic to provide extensive training on raising grievances, the grievance procedure should be covered at induction. Fur-ther, the personnel department should be seen as a source of advice and assistance, and guidance notes can be pre-pared for all the parties, eg managers, representatives, com-panions and workers. (Appendix 2 provides an example of an employee checklist.)

Revise associated documentation

As we have already stated, a new grievance procedure will have implications for the contract of employment. On the assumption that any changes to the existing arrangements have been properly agreed, you must ensure that you revise all associated documentation to remove any anomalies. This includes the statement of terms and conditions, em-ployee handbooks, induction information, equal opportun-ities policies and procedures for dealing with harassment and bullying and other sensitive issues.

Integrate with other management activities

A final but important point is that the new grievance pro-cedure should be fully integrated with other management activities. We will demonstrate this with an example scenario. Imagine that, as a line manager, you have received a formal grievance from an employee alleging that a team leader is frequently heard to make racist comments, some of which are directed at the employee. If, during the period of trying to resolve the grievance, the team leader is due to carry out formal performance reviews with all his team, the disruptive effect of the unresolved grievance would need to be taken into account. For example, you may decide to postpone the performance review meeting for this employee or bring in another person to conduct it. Further, even when the grievance may have been resolved to the employee's satisfaction, eg the team leader is disciplined and recognises the 'error of his (or her) ways', this may be 'only the tip of the iceberg'. In other words, this type of behaviour may be widespread in the organisation, and a wider review and re-education programme may be necessary.

It is also worth pointing out that employing sound management practices should help to prevent grievances. For instance, if you are imposing a new policy, such as a dress code, you must ensure that its contents do not infringe employee rights, eg by discriminating against men or women, or human rights, eg by disadvantaging employees who have unusual dress styles. You should therefore try to make sure that management decisions are based on thorough research and a prediction of reactions, in order to minimise the likelihood of grievances.

Operating grievance procedures

We have, throughout the book, sought to highlight good practices in operating grievance procedures. These are summarised in the table below and some of the points are further demonstrated by case study examples.

Good practice tips
Ensure that the organisational climate and culture is a supportive one
Employ good day-to-day management practices, eg consult fully over proposed changes (see *Case study 4*)
Make special allowances for individuals who are disabled or whose first language is not English
Follow the procedure
Investigate fully
Take notes of investigations and meetings and keep records
Answer all aspects of the grievance (see *Case study 5*)
Identify the root causes
Identify any constraints on possible solutions, eg budgetary considerations, limits of management authority, precedents set in prior similar cases
Think through the consequences of chosen solutions Be prepared to acknowledge and learn from mistakes
Agree and implement workable solutions (see *Case study 6*)
Ensure other necessary follow-up action is taken, eg improve communication materials
Publicise successes
Review the situation after appropriate time intervals

Case study 4 – consult fully over proposed changes

In one organisation the implementation of a new shift pattern resulted in an unusually high number of formal grievances, many from high-performing and long-serving members of staff. An example of one of the complaints was that the alteration in hours meant that the female employee would not be able to attend bingo on a Monday night. As this was her only regular 'night out with the girls', she was understandably aggrieved. An agreement was reached for her to swap shifts with another employee (who was not a bingo fan).

Case study 5 – answer all aspects of the grievance

Grievances may often concern more than one issue and it is tempting to concentrate on those that are deemed, by management, to be the more important ones and to forget or ignore the others. One organisation was faced with a five-point grievance from a disabled worker who claimed that:

- she was being paid less than an able-bodied colleague doing similar work
- there were no fire extinguishers on the premises
- there were no fire exits in the building
- a first-aid kit was not available
- she was concerned about being asked to lock up at night on her own when colleagues were on holiday.

The manager dealing with the case felt that the most important issue was the first one but investigations showed that it was without foundation. In fact, further investigations of all the issues showed that they were either unfounded or based on misconceptions, though one or two problems did emerge. The manager took great care in applying equal weighting to all the issues when she presented her full findings back to the worker. She explained the existing arrangements, how the misconceptions could have arisen and reassured the worker of the changes that had been made to ensure that there would be no future problems, eg clearing passages to fire exits and better labelling of the location of the first-aid kit.

Case study 6 – agree and implement workable solutions
One national organisation decided to merge a number of its factories in order to reduce overheads. The trade unions, though supportive of the future business plans, felt that they were being financed by the merger programme. A collective grievance was raised and a high-profile media campaign was launched against the company action. The grievance progressed through the disputes procedure and, after lengthy discussions, management recognised that imposing the change had been a mistake. An agreement was reached that mergers would still be considered, where there were good business and economic reasons, but that full consultations would take place in each instance. This incident has proved to be something of a landmark in terms of improving employee relations and the organisation and trade unions are now working towards a partnership approach for the future.

Monitoring and evaluation

The final tip in *Good practice tips* above concerned the need to review after each individual grievance, eg by informal discussions to check on feelings or more formal reviews of action points. It is also important to monitor and evaluate the success of the grievance procedure in general terms.

There are a number of monitoring mechanisms that can be used, some of which would entail revisiting the same questions that were addressed at the auditing stage (see above). You would also need to identify any changes or trends in the overall statistics in order to determine whether, say, there are a number of common causes of grievances or the incidence of grievances is centred around particular functions or teams.

These measures would help to determine the effectiveness of the grievance procedure but periodically a major review will be necessary to ensure that it is achieving its aims and objectives (see Chapter 2). Thus employers could check on success by, say, interviewing or issuing questionnaires to individuals who have raised grievances, discussions with union and other employee representatives or carrying out attitude surveys on wider groups of workers. Further measures of the employee relations climate would also be relevant, such as analysing labour turnover and absenteeism figures.

You should, however, be wary of taking statistics at face value. For instance, a rise in the number of formally registered grievances, following the introduction of a new procedure, should not automatically be seen as a sign of failure. It could be indicative of a healthy working environment where employees feel positive and confident about bringing problems and complaints to the attention of their managers.

Finally, the operation of your grievance procedure should be consistently reviewed in the light of recent organisa tional changes, to ensure that it reflects the existing culture and is in line with employment legislation.

Reference

1 SMITH I. *Croner's Personnel in Practice: Employment Digest.* Croner CCH Group Ltd, Issue No. 476. 29 October 1998. p2.

What skills and knowledge are required to handle grievances?

Good practices

Handling grievances is a complex business and great demands are made on the managers involved in carrying out the investigations and conducting the interviews. The figure entitled *The grievance interview* at the end of the chapter provides a step-by-step approach to handling formal grievance interviews, covering the before, during and after stages.

Managers need to acquire a great deal of knowledge and

employ a wide range of skills if they are to be competent in handling grievance situations. However, many managers are inexperienced or lack confidence in handling grievances. Even those who are more experienced complain that each grievance is different and demands a new set of skills. Thus, as we have already said, there is a need to provide appropriate training to all managers. This training should stand them in good stead both in dealing with formal grievances and in the general day-to-day management of their departments and teams.

Skill requirements

The range of skills drawn upon will vary according to the circumstances surrounding the grievance. For instance:

- It may be the case that the employee's grievance is fully justified and a solution that would satisfy all parties is relatively easy to implement, eg a transfer to different duties or a change to the hours of work. Here the manager will primarily need to exercise sound judgement and be decisive.
- In some cases, negotiation skills will be needed so that compromise solutions can be agreed, eg where an employee is dissatisfied when a request for annual leave has been turned down because of staff shortages.
- On occasions, the raising of grievances may unearth poor management practices such as a lack of transparency in allocating overtime. Here the manager handling the grievance will need to be assertive and persuade other managers to make changes. On the other hand, persuasion and

influencing skills may be called upon when managers cannot provide the solutions sought by employees, eg when a request would necessitate a major and unjustifiable change to working methods affecting a group of workers.

- Sometimes employees realise that a solution is not possible for their particular grievance but are relieved to have the opportunity to 'get it off their chests', eg they find it difficult to work with a particular client. Here managers need to adopt counselling skills as well as exercising tact and diplomacy.

Knowledge requirements

Turning now to the knowledge requirements, let us consider a fictional scenario to demonstrate this. Consider the situation where a female employee has been nominated to attend a weekend training event. The employee does not want to go and approaches her immediate manager to complain that she was only given two weeks' notice and cannot arrange adequate childcare. Any line manager faced with this problem will find it difficult to reach a decision that is satisfactory to all parties. On the assumption that the training is necessary and will be expensive to cancel, the manager needs to investigate the following before reaching a decision:

- Does the contract of employment contain a clause referring to 'out-of-hours' training?
- Which legislative acts are relevant here, eg the Sex Discrimination Act 1975 (regarding indirect sex discrimination)?

- What has happened in the past in similar circumstances (ie custom and practice)?
- Has this employee been willing to attend training events in the past?
- What is known about the employee's domestic circumstances?
- Can alternative arrangements be made to accommodate this training?
- What are the likely repercussions of all the possible solutions?

Thus, in general terms, a line manager faced with the task of addressing a grievance, formal or informal, will need to employ any number of the skills listed below and acquire a working knowledge of a range of relevant issues. This is demonstrated in the table below.

Examples of knowledge and skills requirements	
Knowledge	Skills
The grievance procedure and other company policies, procedures and rules	Investigatory and analytical reasoning
Custom and practice	Counselling
The individuals concerned, eg job duties, history of their relationships, personal records re: attendance, disciplinary actions, training, personal circumstances	Written communication for record keeping and report writing

Relevant legislation	Assertiveness, eg saying 'No' when it is appropriate to do so
Relevant clauses in the contract of employment	Judgement, objectivity and decision-making ability
The organisational culture	Negotiating, persuading and influencing
Details of previous grievances that are similar and any precedents set	Tact and diplomacy
Details of actions taken over any previous grievances raised by the employee	Approachability
Limits of own management authority	Facilitating and conciliating
The pros and cons of alternative solutions	Interviewing (see below)
Likely repercussions of the final decision	Monitoring and reviewing

Investigating grievances

There are two main methods of research: interviews and analysing written information. Careful handling of the investigatory stage will benefit the whole process and should help to highlight optimal solutions to grievances.

Effective investigations may also result in grievances being withdrawn because:

- employees now have a better understanding of the problem
- it becomes clear that the grievance is unfounded
- there is nothing to be gained by pursuing it further.

Case study 7 demonstrates the importance of thorough investigations as well as the need to unearth the true causes of grievances and ensure that the aggrieved are not penalised in any way. In summary, investigating managers must be trained to play 'devil's advocate' to ensure that the investigations are as rigorous as possible.

Case study 7 – carry out full investigations

In one small company the general manager was surprised to receive a grievance from a number of employees regarding what appeared to be a relatively trivial incident. The employees were complaining that the new regional manager had, on a recent site visit, gained access to a filing cabinet that they used to store personal effects. The general manager talked to the regional manager who had a valid explanation for opening the cabinet and was unaware that this had invoked any bad feelings.

The general manager's first instinct was to try to close the matter as quickly as possible but, luckily, he decided to interview separately all those who had complained. He discovered that the main instigator was a valued employee who felt that she had been passed over for promotion and she had seized on this opportunity to make life uncomfortable for the new regional manager. She was concerned that she would now be disciplined but was reassured on this point by the general manager.

Consequently, the initial issue was resolved by the regional manager having an informal discussion about the incident with the employees. The general manager then suggested to the 'instigator' that a performance review meeting should be arranged so that they could discuss her career goals and put into place a training and development plan.

Interviewing skills

Many of the skills required to carry out grievance interviews are common to other types of interview, such as selection, appraisal and disciplinary interviews. The purposes of these interviews obviously vary but, as Martin and Jackson[1] say, they all entail the following:

- preparing for the interview
- preparing the environment
- using open and probing questions
- active listening
- maintaining good eye contact
- using appropriate body language
- using silence
- keeping control of the subject matter and timing
- taking notes
- remaining unemotional
- providing clarification
- summarising.

In order to achieve the right tone for the grievance interview, managers need to:

- attempt to establish a rapport
- instil an appropriate measure of formality so that the employee feels the grievance is being taken seriously
- focus on the problem, ie do not attack the person
- be receptive and approachable
- seek to maintain or enhance the employee's self-esteem
- stay calm and in control
- be reasonable and objective
- be factual and unemotional
- encourage the employee to express opinions and make suggestions
- allow for thinking time for both parties.

Before, during and after the interview

The following checklist (adapted from Martin and Jackson[2]) concentrates on handling grievances that have been formally registered. These guidelines, however, should also prove useful for managers wishing to resolve informal complaints.

The Grievance Interview

Before

Ensure you are familiar with the grievance procedure and what happens should you fail to resolve the grievance at this stage.

Request that the worker (or representative, if applicable) provide full details of the grievance, in writing.

Carry out a full investigation. Seek to establish the facts, eg dates, times, places, witnesses.

Request details of the nature of any prior discussions from appropriate line managers.

Question other parties relevant to the grievance.

Consider any information pertinent to the issue raised, eg policy and procedures, statistical information, custom and practice, notes of interviews, written statements, personal records, employment legislation, codes of practice.

Record all the information that you have acquired, ensuring compliance with the Data Protection Act (DPA) 1998.

Inform the worker, preferably in writing, of the subject matter, time, date, location and nature of the interview and the right to be represented/accompanied.

If the worker is disabled or English is not their first language, check whether any special arrangements will be needed at any time during the procedure, eg access facilities, a reader or interpreter.

Check whether a representative/companion and any witnesses (for either party) will be present and arrange for their release from duties, if applicable. Be prepared to agree a postponement to the interview should individuals be unavailable.

Arrange a suitable venue for the interview, ie a quiet place free from interruptions, and allow sufficient time in your diary.

Ensure that the meeting will be properly constituted, according to the procedure.

During

Convene the grievance interview.

Listen objectively to the worker's complaint.

Regardless of the eventual outcome of the grievance, thank the worker for bringing the matter to your attention.

Hear witness evidence and allow for examination and cross examination, as appropriate, by both sides. Consider any documentation provided by the worker.

Be prepared to answer questions/explain current practices, etc.

Seek clarification of the key issues, including
any solutions sought.
Summarise your understanding throughout the interview.

Arrange for comprehensive notes to be taken.

Allow time for the worker to confer in private with his or her
representative/companion at any point in the proceedings

Adjourn the interview to allow consideration of the
points raised and the circumstances. If the case is
particularly complex or further investigations are necessary,
request and agree an extension to the time allowed
before a response is expected.

Consider the appropriate action to be taken, if any, bearing
in mind any relevant procedures and possible repercussions.

Reconvene and inform the worker of your decision,
giving your reasons and seeking agreement, if possible.
If an immediate recommendation cannot be given,
ensure that it is communicated to both parties within the
appropriate timescale.

If a mutually acceptable agreement has not been/is not likely
to be reached, inform the worker of his or her right to
progress to the next stage and the procedure for so doing.

Afterwards

Record the results and write up the notes of the interview. Arrange for confirmation of the decision to be sent to the worker and representative/companion. In the interests of good employee relations and, bearing in mind data protection provisions, you may wish to publicise the resultant changes to all workers.

Monitor the situation by, for example, maintaining informal contact with the worker or arranging a formal review meeting (whichever is most appropriate).

Evaluate the success or otherwise of any actions that have been taken as a result of the grievance being raised.

A final case study demonstrates a point that was raised in Chapter 1 of this book, ie that managers should welcome and encourage grievances as they can be useful tools in highlighting the need for revision of management policies, procedures and/or practices.

Case study 8 – welcome and encourage grievances
Many managers dread grievances and either look for a short-term fix or try to avoid dealing with them at all. But effective handling of grievances can help to identify poor practices and may reduce the likelihood of employment tribunal claims in the future.

One national company received a complaint from a

part-time worker about a perceived lack of training and promotion opportunities. The initial response might have been to say that this was unfounded as the organisation prided itself on its family-friendly working practices. Nevertheless, subsequent investigations, including interviewing the complainant, revealed company documents stating that eligibility for entry to the Management Development Programme was dependent on working a minimum number of hours. This restriction was immediately removed, in the light of current legislation, and the whole question of opportunities for part-timers was fully reviewed.

References

1 MARTIN M. *and* JACKSON T. *Personnel Practice.* London, Chartered Institute of Personnel and Development, 2000. p115.
2 *Ibid.*, p118.

What are the key points?

1　There is no statutory obligation for employers to provide a grievance procedure, but there is an implied term in the contract of employment that employees must have a means of raising grievances, in order to seek redress, without fear of reprisal.

2　Recent changes in legislation, the new ACAS Code of Practice and good practice initiatives highlight the need for formal workplace procedures and there is a new statutory right of accompaniment for workers.

3　The content and scope of grievance procedures will depend on a number of factors including the nature, size and culture of the organisation, whether it is unionised or not, and the existence of related policies and procedures.

4　Grievance procedures should conform to a hierarchical structure and a staged approach, involving an informal stage and a right of appeal to higher levels of management.

5　Managers should not view grievances as a nuisance but should welcome them and encourage employees to raise any concerns they have about the workplace. One of the main benefits of effective grievance handling is that it can help to foster healthy employee relations.

6   It should be possible to resolve the majority of employee complaints before they become formal grievances. This should be done swiftly, fairly and locally, and to the satisfaction of all concerned.

7   The existence of good management practices, eg effective communication mechanisms and employee involvement schemes, should result in fewer misconceptions and misunderstandings and, therefore, fewer grievances.

8   Managers must carry out full and impartial investigations of grievances and seek to identify the root causes.

9   Training and/or guidance should be available to all parties who play a role in the grievance procedure, but managers, especially, require intensive training in order to develop the requisite skills needed to handle grievances effectively.

10 Where a solution is possible, managers should agree and implement workable solutions. Promises must be kept.

What else do we need to know?

> ☑ Further reading
> ☑ Useful contacts

Listed below are some suggestions for further reading and useful contacts.

Further reading

The following ACAS publications are available from ACAS Reader (Tel. 01455 852225):

Code of Practice on Disciplinary and Grievance Procedures. May 2000.
Self Help Guide. Producing Disciplinary and Grievance Procedures. July 1999.
Guide for Small Firms. Dealing with Grievances. November 1997.
The Role of ACAS. August 1999.
Preventing and Resolving Collective Disputes. July 1999.
Providing Information and Advice. July 1999.
Individual Employment Rights. September 1998.

Other useful publications include:

INDUSTRIAL SOCIETY *Managing Best Practice: Managing Discipline and Grievance*. No. 57. London, Industrial Society, March 1999.

PPI TRAINING CONSULTANTS *Handling Employees' Problems and Complaints*. Cambridgeshire, Fenman, 1996.

Useful contacts

Advisory, Conciliation and Arbitration Service (ACAS). There are 11 regional public enquiry points – see your telephone directory.

Centre for Dispute Resolution (CEDR). A leading international organisation in the field of Alternative Dispute Resolution. Tel. 020 7600 0500.
E-mail: mediate@cedr.co.uk
Website: www.cedr.co.uk

Chartered Institute of Personnel and Development (CIPD, formerly IPD). Tel: 020 8971 9000.
E-mail: cipd@cipd.co.uk
Website: www.cipd.co.uk

Citizen Advice Bureaux. Locally based – see your telephone directory.

Public Concern at Work (regarding whistleblowing). Tel: 020 7404 6609.
E-mail: whistle@pcaw.demon.co.uk
Website: www.pcaw.demon.co.uk

Appendix 1: Example joint procedure

Barnet and Chase Farm Hospitals NHS Trust: Policy on managing individual grievances and collective disputes

(© Barnet and Chase Farms Hospital NHS Trust)

1.0 Principles

1.1 The Trust believes that the opportunity to raise grievances, both individually and collectively, is essential to the development of constructive employee relations.

1.2 Such grievances, if resolved rapidly, fairly and as close to the point of origin as possible, will benefit staff and managers and be in the interests of the Trust.

1.3 Any member of staff who raises a grievance in good faith, will not suffer any detrimental treatment for bringing the matter to the attention of management, even if the grievance is not substantiated.

1.4   The procedure will be applied fairly and consistently to all staff employed by the Trust, regardless of personal characteristics or employment status.

1.5   Matters relating to equal opportunities, harassment or concerns regarding the working capabilities or practices of other staff may be raised under this policy, or under other policies reserved for those specific matters e.g.:

1.5.1 the Policy on Equal Opportunities and Non-Discrimination

1.5.2 the Policy on Avoidance and Treatment of Harassment

1.5.3 and any prevailing policies on whistleblowing or raising staff concerns.

1.6   All matters of this nature will be considered highly confidential and discussion with other parties will only be acceptable where they are clearly within the procedure.

2.0 Representation

2.1   A member of staff may have representation from a trade union representative or work colleague within the Trust, neither of which may act in a legal capacity, at any time during the procedure.

3.0 Definitions

3.1   A grievance is any problem or concern raised by an individual employee.

3.2   A dispute is any problem or concern raised by a group of employees, collectively.

3.3 The line manager is intended to mean the immediate manager of the employee, whatever his/her post title.

3.4 The Head of Department is usually a senior manager who has responsibility for the ward/department or area in which the employee works.

3.5 The term 'days' refers to working days and the term 'weeks' refers to working weeks, on the basis that Monday to Friday are working days.

3.6 Throughout the policy, any reference to 'grievance' will be taken to imply 'grievance' or 'dispute'.

4.0 Informal procedures

4.1 Employees are encouraged to raise individual problems or concerns with their immediate line manager on a one to one basis, usually within five working days, with a view to resolving any difficulties as quickly and as informally as possible.

4.2 Members of staff should be prepared to allow their line manager up to five working days to consider the nature of the problem and to consider the possible solutions before engaging the formal procedure.

4.3 If the matter is of a personal nature or relates to the line manager directly, the employee may not wish to discuss the matter with the line manager and may raise the issue with his/her Human Resources Officer who may agree to contact the line manager on his/her behalf in an attempt to resolve the matter informally.

5.0 Formal procedure

5.1 Stage One

5.1.1 If the matter has not been resolved through informal discussions with the line manager, the member of staff may raise a formal grievance or dispute by completing a 'notification of grievance or dispute' form (appendix 1 [see page 87]) and sending this to the Head of Department, with a copy to the Human Resources Manager who will coordinate all stages of the procedure.

5.1.2 The Head of Department will consider the matter and try to resolve the issue through a formal hearing within two weeks of receiving the notification from the employee.

5.1.3 If the matter has not been resolved to the employee's satisfaction through a formal hearing with the Head of Department, the employee has the right to refer the matter to the appropriate Director (clinical or non-clinical).

5.2 Stage Two

5.2.2 The Director will consider the matter and try to resolve the issue through a formal hearing.

5.2.3 If the matter is not resolved to the employee's satisfaction through a formal hearing at this level, the employee has the right to refer the matter to a Grievance/Disputes Committee which will be the final level of this procedure.

5.3 Stage Three

5.3.2 The Grievance/Disputes Committee will be chaired

by an independent chair, nominated by ACAS, with a Non-Executive Director from the Trust Board, and a Full Time Officer of a Trade Union. None of the Committee members will have had any previous involvement with the case.

5.3.3   The matter will be considered through a formal hearing which will be convened, wherever possible, within one calendar month.

6.0 Timings

6.1   Grievance hearings will be arranged through the Human Resources Department within ten working days of receipt of the 'notification of grievance or dispute' form. This time limit should only be extended in exceptional circumstances and by agreement between all parties.

6.2   Decisions reached by the person hearing the grievance (the Grievance Officer) will be confirmed in writing no later than five working days subsequent to the grievance hearing.

6.3   If the employee decides to take the matter to the next level, he/she will confirm this in writing (or on the 'notification of grievance or dispute' form, if preferred) to the relevant line manager, copied to the Human Resources Manager, within 10 working days of receipt of the confirmation of the earlier decision.

6.4   Although every effort will be made to keep to the time limits referred to, these may be extended at any stage by mutual agreement, or where the specified manager or trade union representative is unavailable within the time limits, and where the aggrieved party insists on the nominated person rather than a deputy.

7.0 Management of the process

7.1 Formal grievance procedures will be coordinated by the Trust Human Resources Department which will:

7.1.1 Attend to all arrangements relating to the hearing(s) in accordance with the policy.

7.1.2 Arrange to act as secretary to the hearing.

7.2 The secretary to the hearing will:

7.2.1 Advise the officer/panel conducting the hearing on all matters relevant to the grievance including the procedure at the hearing and the appropriateness of the submissions.

7.2.2 Ensure that the hearing is conducted fairly and consistently in accordance with the Trust policy and procedure.

7.2.3 Take notes and make the notes available to both sides following the meeting.

7.2.4 Ask clarifying questions at the hearing if he/she thinks it appropriate.

8.0 Circulation of documents

8.1 The following documents should be forwarded to the Human Resources Manager no later than five working days before the scheduled grievance hearing. The designated Human Resources Manager will circulate copies to the officer hearing the grievance or members of the grievance committee, the management representative, the employee and the employee's representative.

8.2   Manager's Statement

8.2.1   The statement should present the circumstances of the case, and should include a full set of the key documents to be presented at the hearing. A copy of the employee's job description should be included if appropriate. Wherever possible the Manager should address the specific points raised by the employee through the 'notification of grievance' form.

8.3   Employee's Statement

8.3.1   This statement may be prepared in conjunction with the representative and will state the reasons why the grievance has been lodged or is being pursued. The statement should also include the reasons for disagreement to the response offered by the line manager on an informal basis or through an earlier grievance hearing.

9.0 Status quo

9.1   The status quo (i.e. the working and management arrangements which apply at the time the procedure commences) will operate until the procedures have been exhausted. Where it is believed that the status quo contravenes overriding obligations, e.g. duty of care to patients, advice will be sought from the Medical or Nursing Directors.

10.0 Procedure at the hearing

10.1   The procedure at the hearing or appeal is outlined in Appendix II [see page 88].

11.0 Liaison with human resources

11.1   Managers will take advice from and involve a Human Resources Officer at all stages of the procedure.

11.2   Staff and their representatives shall have recourse to a Human Resources Officer for clarification, information and interpretation of the procedure at any time.

12.0 Interpreters

12.1   Where an interpreter is required, an interpreter will be provided by the Trust and must be acceptable to both sides. If satisfactory arrangements cannot be made prior to the proposed hearing, the hearing may be deferred until an appropriate interpreter can be sought.

13.0 Review

13.1   This policy will be reviewed two years from the date of agreement and every two years thereafter.

Appendix I

NOTIFICATION OF GRIEVANCE OR DISPUTE _____ STAGE

Strictly Confidential

To: _____   Copy: _____
Head of Department   Human Resources Manager

From: _____   Job title: _____

Department: _____   Line Manager: _____

Trade Union: _____   Nominated Rep: _____

Substance of Grievance

Please detail the substance of your grievance and attach
any related correspondence, if appropriate.

Signed: _____   Date: _____

Please send this form to your Head of Department and a copy to Human Resources

This grievance will be acknowledged by the Human Resource Department upon receipt,
after which it will be dealt with in accordance with procedures outlined in the Trust
Policy on Managing Individual Grievances and Collective Disputes, a copy of which will
be sent with the acknowledgment as a matter of course.

Appendix II

Procedure at the Grievance or Dispute Hearing

1. The employee or his/her representative will state the case of the employee and call any witnesses.
2. The Officer/Grievance Committee and the Management representative will be entitled to ask questions of the individual and any witnesses called.
3. The employee may re-examine his/her witness on any matters referred to in the examination by the Officer/Committee or Management representative.
4. The Management representative will state his/her case and call any witnesses.
5. The Officer/Grievance Committee and the employee or his/her representative will be entitled to ask questions of the individual and any witnesses called.
6. The Management representative may re-examine his/her witness on any matters referred to in their examination by the Officer/Committee or employee or his/her representative.
7. The Management representative will sum up his/her case.
8. The employee or his/her representative will sum up his/her case.
9. Nothing in the foregoing procedure will prevent the Officer/Committee from inviting the representative of either party to clarify or amplify any statement he/she may have made.
10. The Officer/Committee may, at their discretion, adjourn a hearing in order that further information or evidence may be produced by either party. Requests for

adjournments will not be unreasonably refused.

11. The Officer/Committee will consider his/its recommendation in private. If an immediate recommendation cannot be given, it will be communicated in writing to both parties within five days of the hearing by the secretary.

Appendix 2: Example guidance notes

Extract from NCH Action for Children Grievance Policy and Procedure: Employees' checklist

(© NCH Action for Children)

- Have you done *everything* within your power to resolve your problem or complaint informally with your line manager?
- If, after raising your concern with your line manager, you remain dissatisfied and wish to use the Grievance Procedure, write down briefly what your complaint is, keep a copy and give the other copy to your line manager.
- If your complaint is with the behaviour of your line manager, keep a copy of your written complaint, give a copy to your line manager and send a copy to your Director of Social Work, Director of Appeals or Head of Department.
- Consider the nature of support you would like and whether you wish to invite another employee or a representative of a professional association or

trade union to accompany you to your meeting
with the manager considering your grievance.

- Consider whether any issues should be raised in
  your supervision or at team meetings.
- You may find it helpful to write down in detail the
  thoughts and feelings you have about your
  grievance. You will not then be relying on your
  memory alone.
- Before you meet the manager considering your
  grievance, decide on the role you wish anyone
  accompanying you to play at the meeting.
- You may wish to seek advice from the personnel
  department.
- If a meeting is arranged, agree a venue that is
  comfortable for you.

Appendix 3: Example flowchart

Extract from Ipswich Borough Council's Disciplinary and Grievance Procedure: Employee's guide

(© Ipswich Borough Council)

Ipswich Borough Council grievance procedure

Procedure steps	Action	Timescale
1st stage Discuss the matter with your service manager. If the problem is outside the scope of your supervisor he/she will refer you to an alternative person to hear your initial complaint	Your service manager or the alternative person will give an oral reply	➤ Within seven days
2nd stage If you are dissatisfied with the reply you have the right to consult a representative of your choice, eg a trade union representative, who may take the matter up with the service manager either on your behalf or in conjunction with you	Your service manager will give an oral reply	➤ Within seven days
3rd stage If you continue to be aggrieved, you or your representative must submit your grievance in writing to your service manager who will forward it to your corporate director. You should retain a copy of the grievance submission	Your corporation director will arrange a meeting with all interested parties including, where appropriate, your representative. You will receive written confirmation of the meeting	➤ Within seven days
4th stage If you are still aggrieved you will be allowed by the council to continue your complaint to an Appeals Committee of Members	The Appeal Committee will confirm their decision in writing to you	

Chartered Institute of Personnel and Development

Customer Satisfaction Survey

We would be grateful if you could spend a few minutes answering these questions and return the postcard to CIPD. Please use a black pen to answer. If you would like to receive a free CIPD pen, please include your name and address. IPD MEMBER Y/N

....

1. Title of book ....

2. Date of purchase: month .... year ....

3. How did you acquire this book?
☐Bookshop ☐Mail order ☐Exhibition ☐Gift ☐Bought from Author

4. If ordered by mail, how long did it take to arrive:
☐1 week ☐2 weeks ☐more than 2 weeks

5. Name of shop .... Town.. Country...........

6. Please grade the following according to their influence on your purchasing decision with 1 as least influential: (please tick)

	1	2	3	4	5
Title					
Publisher					
Author					
Price					
Subject					
Cover					

7. On a scale of 1 to 5 (with 1 as poor & 5 as excellent) please give your impressions of the book in terms of: (please tick)

	1	2	3	4	5
Cover design					
Paper/print quality					
Good value for money					
General level of service					

8. Did you find the book:
Covers the subject in sufficient depth ☐Yes ☐No
Useful for your work ☐Yes ☐No

9. Are you using this book to help:
☐In your work ☐Personal study ☐Both ☐Other (please state)

Please complete if you are using this as part of a course

10. Name of academic institution..

11. Name of course you are following? ....

12. Did you find this book relevant to the syllabus? ☐Yes ☐No ☐Don't know

Thank you!

To receive regular information about CIPD books and resources call 020 8263 3387.

1795/05/00

2

Publishing Department

Chartered Institute of Personnel and Development

CIPD House

Camp Road

Wimbledon

London

SW19 4BR